Mankind in universe

Art d'Hommage
Lyrics

Poems by Rainer Dahlhaus
Paintings by Angelika Dahlhaus

Inauguration

With the series „Art d'Hommage literature" will be opened a sequence of scriptures from the fields of philosophie, lyrics and art, with the aim of to unite people of different nations and cultures all over the world.

The intention and the „how" of this interconnection is prefigured in the respective foreword and introduction. It is our objective to translate the scriptures in several languages to strengthen the unifying bond of a common spiritual world.

In addition to the poetic texts the images of artistic works should contribute to this emerging weave of humanity. The artist has been working for many years with discovered artefacts from all cultures since the dawn of humanity (cave painting , rock engravings).
The artistic procession of these motifs reflects the genuine and common roots of mankind and indicates at the same time, that art can achieve excellent service to discover this - entirely in the spirit of the author of the great and famous ode „To joy" - Friedrich Schiller:
„..be embraced millions..."

In this sense the first print will go into publication related with the desire, that people of all cultures in the world shall be involved in the formation and strengthening of this devine ligament.

Bibliografische Information der Deutschen Nationalbibliothek. Die Deutsche Nationalbibliothek verzeichnet diese Publikation in der Deutschen Nationalbibliografie, detaillierte bibliografische Daten sind im Internet über http://dnb.dnb.de abrufbar

© 2016 Rainer Dahlhaus

Herstellung und Verlag:
BoD - Books on demand, Norderstedt

ISNB: 9783743142329

Introduction

What we are currently experencing and
learn is a vast world crisis -
a human crisis -
as only occurs in changing times.
This crisis causes a
comprehensive transformation,
which can be referred with the word
„cataclysm" -
at the end with a new constellation
of huge significance.
The technical developement
on the one hand -
humans responsibility awareness
on the other
are grown into a menacing imbalance.
This increasing tense relationship
can only be surmount
by a radically altered
consciousness mutation.

Two areas of tension dominates
the current situation in the world -
we have a raising of individualism
with a self-centered character,
that wants all and everything.

At the same time we have
an extreme collectivism
with a character of insolence -
even hybris -
masses tendency with the feeling
„to be is everything".

Here there is an overestimation
of the individual
attached to a profiling obsession
without limit -
there is an entire disparagement
of the individual,
in which it is rated only as a mere number.
This dual splitting rules and tenses
all societies up to destructive
manifestations.

The overcoming of this
disastrous „electric" field
is only possible if we as self
inaugerate and advance an
extension and intensification
of our consciousness -
this actually in two directions -
towards the self -
including its origin, present and future -
and towards the „You" - embracing the
world, nature and all creatures.

So we learn to sharpen the eyes
for the strong seed of the „New"
and burgeoning -
for the subversive world
forms the humus.
This is the ongoing mutation,
in which we live now -
just in the middle.

From this ethos and contemplations
the following lyric should be taken
and perhaps be effectively.
The collection of these poems
wants to make a modest contribution
to draw and display
some new ways of thinking and feeling.

In the author's opinion
Art represents an universal
connecting element,
for its deep and true understanding
the heart should not be set aside.

Encouragement

From the force
that binds all beings,
he is set free,
who surmounts himself.

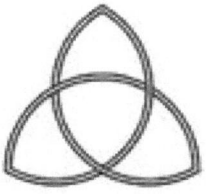

You would not seek me -
if you had not found me

Origin - ending

That you can not end - that makes you grand
and that you
never start - that is your fate -
your hymn is spinning
like stellar vault -
origin - ending - all time the same -
the center reveals what remains
at the end - and initially was.

The source

The source - cryptic - as if nothing, free - effective
from itself, formless - and yet full of magic force.
It nourishes
everything, but these know
nothing about - he that discernes
this well - traces nature at all.

Devine merging

Beauty - as gen'ral - rainbow - as particular
phenomenon merges heaven with earth in
virtous and
sensual way. -
Rejoice to this
splendid mediation means
to dwell in the essenc of life.

Thoughts and fate

The human being look upon his fate as an
outside, because the inner junction is concealed.
However the soul
includes ev'ry occurence,
for this are purely the thoughts
projected outwards - about what
we ask ourselves -
it always is
granted to us.

As nature

As nature in its diversity reveals one
and only spirit essence - so in whole of
art realm their
weaves and seems a lovely sense
of eternal mode -this is the
meaning of the truth, which adorns
itselve with blossoms of life and
looks upon a lightfull heart.

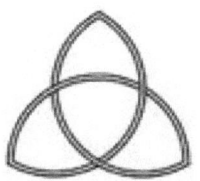

A veritable art work

A veritable art work for our mind remains
as a nature creation - intangible - not
visible in core.
It is considered, perceived -
it come across - but really can
not be dicerned and hard to be
described in words.

Sunlit gate

Merely through
the sunlit gate
you will achieve
the realm of truth.

What we perceive
as beauty here,
we once will face
as solemn sooth.

The world is one

Joy and love -
Heavenly rays -
Weaving stars
Floating through space -
Magic scent
Filling the air -
Fire blessing
Spirited glare.
Be embraced
You billion souls -
Beyond the stars
The golden bowls
Are filled with joy,
With love and faith -
The world is one
In eternal grace.

Blueprint of god

*In ocean - wide and vast - you as a drop will close
yourself? - so you will never merge to a pearl -
even the floods
will shake you and rush - so
open your innermost organs
and mingle with all the streams -
full joy and pain, which flows through you -
you serve yourself for blueprint god.*

Dignity of planet earth

The dignity of this planet earth is delivered
into your hand - beware of it ! This treasure
wanes with you -
with you it will increase.
The holy magic of poetries
serves a wise plan of the world -
so lead the prosperous life
into greatest harmony.

―――――

Silent Yard

All in life replays - forever young is only
fantasy. - What never and nowhere proceeds,
that never gets
obsolete.
In sacred silent yard of heart
you have to flee from urge of life. -
Freedom only is in realm of dream and beauty
blooms just in a chant.

Emergent life

In common creation no destruction occurs
without invisible segment newly be formed.
Ev'ry decline
aims to a new formation -
every death paves the way to
pure emergent life

Aeons across

All you discern as reality and as truth
did you already know as forever and now -
Aeons across -
a variety of messages
always available for you -
the double-sided coin is one !

The lines of life

The lines of life are true diverse as ways and path
and mountains edge - what we are here on planet
earth
yonder a god
will aim to amend this life
into freedom and joy for all.

Contemplation

Contemplation is the innermost core of an
honest and real insight and every new-
found verity
is the benificial yield
of fraternal liaision with
this insight integral force.

Sublime glance

So resign the thoughts on a sheet - innocent white,
the sublime yet glance over the shoulder -
you're right -
past ... vitality ...
the unborn and unformed life.
Blessed the one who feel how to
blossom and thrive.

As a mirror

The wise beholds his heart as a mirror - dosn't
seek the things - neither go to meet - what acts on him
he takes it all
in his brilliant face - but not
involved to keep it.
This enables him to triumph
about all and not to be
even injured.

Go straight

Go straight as the trees - live your life as strong as the
mountains - be gentle as the wind in spring - preserve
the warmth of sun
in your heart - feel butterflies
wings as a wave in your soul -
so the spirit of earth is yours.

Humans desire

Humans desire are like arrows of light -
they can discover dreams, visit the land of soul,
cure illness and
pain - scare away dread and fear
and even create in a force
the ground as the sun and the stars.

Language of true heart

You know that trees can talk ? - they speak to you
if you listen - they converse about the life in
past and future -
about joy and love , pain and
sorrow - at any rate they speak
on earth the language of true heart.

Nature renews

Nature renews all the time - thousand of days
that pass - return in a new and singular frame.
Learn to embrace
eternity in ev'ry
moment - this aeons minute is
like a pure immutable jewel
in the heart of a deep wide world.

Power of thoughts

The power of thoughts is invisible as
a core in ground, a grant tree arises from.
This giant force
is the spring of emerging
changes in profound humans life.

Sky and roots

It is well for man to have his head in the clouds
and with thoughts dwell with the eagles - but he
has to
remember that
a tree that skyward grows
also its roots has to sprout
deep in the heart of mother earth.

Stones speak

Stones speak softly - and only in a whisper -
they talk about their fate - only those can hear
the gentle voice,
who are able to listen
the swoosh of the wind - the floating
of clouds - and the mellow swaying
of blossoms and leafs - .
Can you raise these mysteries all ?

Take your time

Take your time to look at the sky - behold the
figures in soft white clouds - listen to the ways of
the blowing wind -
feel the glacial water and
walk with quiet and cautious steps. -
We are intruders - tolerated from
infinite universe for only a
short time.

Fortunate thoughts

There is a relationship and friendship between
fortunate thoughts and presents of the moment -
both fall down from
heaven and touch you inside -
so you know in your heart is God
as the fragrance rest in the bloom.

If no wind stirs up

If no wind stirs up some waves around your heart -
all you see are just blue mountains and green trees -
but if inside
things are in motion - all here
you will see hovering birds and
jumping fish - musing snails
and bustling ants.

Mirror

How the sun and the moon
can not mirror in muddy water -
so the allmighty force
can not shine in a heart
turned grey by living
only in thoughts of „me" and „I".

The world is like a chessboard

The world is like a chessboard - splayed day and night,
where fate moves the people back and forth - to and fro,
announces chess -
strikes and at the end - in turn
place them straight - inescapable
in a standing by wooden box.

Timeless symbols

Flowers are the timeless symbols of profound truth.
Its scent provides an unspoken message - its
transient beauty
mediates a sense for the
passing lanes of life - and blooming
stands for real return of God.

———

A single word

A single word -
spoken with solid belief -
with honesty -
true - without concerns and grief
while looking face to face -
centered with eyes -
so all the sayings
scare away lies.
This single moment -
a strong light ray -
all written words
will blow away.

Change holds the might

Every blossom will get fruit -
every morning night.
Nothing on earth is eternal,
only change holds the might.

Even the beautiful summer
feels the fading and fall -
so leaf, be patient, stay still,
when wind will send you a call.

Play your game - not defend
yourself and let it pass.
The wind, he will carry you
home - no more - no less.

Enjoy

The mirror of nature
is the clearest of all -
enjoy the glance!
Only the beauty will rescue
the bad threaten ball -
enjoy and dance !

Love and faith

Just because
humans believe
in immortality -
love can be
and shine.
With dissolving
of faith -
love would be
extinguished too.

Spread out your wings

Once - thousand of
years ago
a dear homeland
there was -
a garden, where from
white birds grave
the snowdrops glance.

Spread out your wings,
flee the space
that lines your life -
fly down
to the times
of those gold,
that shines
to your heart
evermore.

Human being

Human being
is a mysterie
you have to decipher -
and if you do
for an age -
don't say
you lost time -
for solving
this secret means -
being human.

―――-

Humility

The highness of a human soul
is partly appreciate
at the level of
how much - and when
it is able to witness
humility and devotion
in a true
and honest wise.

Mystic awareness

Much on earth is concealed - but we are applied with
the mystic awareness of a vibrant bond - for
thoughts and feelings
are rooted in far-off worlds.
All vitality emerged from
touch with variant spheres beyond.

In the depths

He that will behold
the living god
face to face -
should not look
for his world
of thoughts
at an empty
firmament -
but already
in the depths
of his own true soul.

Noble duty

*To know responsible in respect to universe -
at every moment - and to commit yourself
against weakness,
falsehood, lies and timidness -
to prove oneself as brother and
friend to all creation - goodness
without being weak - clemency
without being faint - thats it!*

Psyche

Obviously we are just transitional nature
and our terrestrial presence evidently
is the progress
as a caterpillar which
transmutes soundless and small into
a light and lovely butterfly.

Our thoughts

Thoughts are like objects - with body, breath and
wings
our innermost ideas rush to the hidden
places of the world
and left their lanes - so we build
our future unknowingly
and our fate is what we think.

Right wave

Thoughts - once escaped
are immortal . -
The ether is an
infinite reservoir
for ideas
and we are able
to fish out -
if we receive
the right
resonant
wave.

Royal soul

He is prosperous and full of royal dignity,
who knows how much donation and spirited force
harbors the ground,
the waters, the plants and the air
and who knows how these treasures
arise and fade - but never want
to hold on
its life.

The best

The great day and crowning festival of life comes,
when the third eye gets clear the essence of nature
and spirit of god. -
If you realize, that all
what exist has to be - should be
and that it is even - the best.

———-

Time

Time is too slow
for those who wait -
too fast for those
who fear -
too long for mourners,
too short for joyers -
whereas for those
with hearty love
the hours stand
for eternity -
what ever
life yields.

Spheric blessings

Doubt is reluctance, contraction, cold and ice -
Faith is expansion, attraction, warmth and sun -
summer absorbs
the spears of light and golden
fruits find their abundance suffused
with the spheric blessings of god.

The greatest good

The greatest and invaluable good of man
is the knowing and feeling of himself - who
missed it short time
and gather again - just he
knows all its worth and will do
ev'rything for never to lose.

Clean your eyes

Everyone simply walk his lane - if waste or blase - whats to you ? - what does the fire in winter cold ?
It sparkles and glows.
What does the tree the one forgets ?
It blooms and grows - therefore
each practice as before.
Clean your eyes - be silent -stay well !

Echo chant

Luminous thoughts

*Thoughts are like
flowing water -
however
sculptured through art,
structured in
excellence form -
they become a
luminous diamond*